Go & Grow!

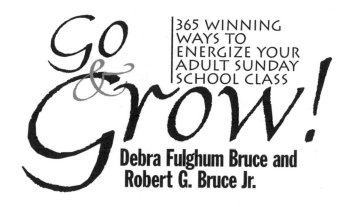

Go

365 WINNING WAYS TO ENERGIZE YOUR ADULT SUNDAY SCHOOL CLASS

& Grow!

Debra Fulghum Bruce and Robert G. Bruce Jr.

Abingdon Press / Nashville

GO AND GROW!
365 WINNING WAYS TO ENERGIZE YOUR ADULT SUNDAY SCHOOL CLASS

Copyright © 1998 by Abingdon Press

This book is printed on recycled, acid-free, elemental-chlorine–free paper.

ISBN 0-687-06024-9

Scripture quotations, unless otherwise indicated, are from the New Revised Standard Version Bible, copyright © 1989, by the Division of Christian Education of the National Council of the Churches of Christ in the United States of America.

98 99 00 01 02 03 04 05 06 07—10 9 8 7 6 5 4 3 2 1

MANUFACTURED IN THE UNITED STATES OF AMERICA

If you've ever dreamed of having a growing Sunday school class, if you have little time during the week to nurture your class and have noticed that attendance and enthusiasm have diminished in the past months, if you are searching for quick yet meaningful ways to let members know that someone cares, if you need practical tips to strengthen your own spiritual pilgrimage, then the suggestions in this book will inspire, energize, and motivate you to go and grow! This book will help you turn those dreams and thoughts into energy and evangelism as you use the 365 winning ways to increase attendance and participation as well as personal desire to respond to God's Word.

In our harried, fast-paced society, creativity in the Sunday school classroom is more important now than ever before as you relate the gospel message in a manner that meets the needs of class members. Creativity is also important as you set goals for class growth. This involves devising ongoing innovative ideas and methods that will inspire, encourage, and motivate active and inactive members to attend class week after week and become a vital part of this fellowship.

During the numerous seminars we lead across the nation, we have spent a *great deal of time talking with teachers of every age group about their specific faith and classroom needs. Most say, "We want motivating ideas, but we don't have time to do more than one idea at a time." In a society where people are over-ly committed with kids, careers, and chaos, and where people are searching for "quick fixes," easy-to-follow tips such as the ones found in this book are the most helpful and usable for busy teachers.*

We've given you 365 practical and inspirational tips—one idea or inspiration a day—to boost enthusiasm and caring in the classroom with the optimal goal of increasing growth—both quantitatively and qualitatively. Each quick and easy tip will give you added insight into how to become more evangelistic in your classroom, as well as in your personal life. Once you have gone through each of the 365 ideas, turn back to idea #1 and once again renew your commitment to nurture and energize yourself and your class.

So, what are we waiting for? Let's get started with some winning ways to create new enthusiasm for Jesus Christ in your classroom and in your life.

1

Make plans for weekly fellowship time. Plan a short, informal gathering before class where members can greet one another. Ask two members to welcome newcomers and introduce them to others. Take turns each week providing beverages and snacks. Provide name tags for members and visitors.

2

Organize for evangelism. On separate cards, write pertinent information about class members, such as name, address, home and work phone numbers, birth date, anniversary date, and personal interests. Keep the cards in a recipe file box, and refer to them weekly as you reach out to members in different ways to energize your Sunday school class.

3

Be a shepherd. In John 10:3*b*, we read, "And the sheep hear his voice. He calls his own sheep by name and leads them out." As you teach the Word of God, remember also to be a shepherd who helps to heal the wounds, celebrate the victories, and provide members with opportunities for response.

4

Record prayer requests. Take blank sheets of paper and envelopes to class this week. Before the lesson, ask each member to write down three prayer requests and seal them in an envelope. After three months, open the letters and ask members to read them. How were their prayers answered? Remind your class that God sometimes says "yes," "wait," "I'll surprise you!" as well as "no" to prayer requests.

5

Start a daily spiritual journal or diary. In an inexpensive spiral notebook, use confessional writing to capture your deepest feelings and thoughts, which you might not feel comfortable sharing aloud. Record prayer lists, note answers to prayers, and set personal goals in your journal. Keep your Bible and daily devotional guide close at hand and focus on scripture strengths to help you maintain control when life seems most harried.

6

Become an inviting class. Studies report that more than 82 percent of new members join a church because someone invited them to attend. Encourage members to bring friends, neighbors, and relatives to Sunday school.

7

Carefully read and outline the lesson material each week. Read what the author is saying, underline the main points, and mark ideas about which you have questions. As you methodically work through your curriculum lesson and study the weekly message, you will become more familiar with the material, and on Sunday morning you will be able to share the message by using your own words.

8

Focus on the scriptures. Use Bible commentaries such as *The Interpreter's Bible* or *Barclay's Commentary* to bring new insight to your lesson.

9

Watch your body language when teaching. Body stance, posture, and facial expressions assist the spoken word in disseminating the message. Practice in front of a mirror or with family members to develop your personal teaching style.

10

Start a monthly class newsletter. Ask a volunteer to write the newsletter. Personalize the material with information such as lesson topics, joys and concerns, prayer requests, and upcoming social events. Photocopy, and mail the newsletter to all members and visitors.

11

Establish teaching goals. Goals help turn dreams into reality. Without them you have no guidelines by which to measure growth—quantitatively or qualitatively. Think about your goals today and write them down.

12

Let others know what you are teaching. Print your lesson topic in the church newsletter or in the Sunday bulletin. This will inform people who do not attend Sunday school of what your class is discussing each week.

13

Take advantage of teacher training events. Many workshops and conferences are available through area churches or denominational offices. If none are available, order or purchase books and resources on how to teach more effectively.

14

Identify your fears about teaching. Spend time talking with other teachers about them. Do you worry about mispronouncing a biblical term or misquoting a pertinent passage of Scripture? If you can identify your fears early on, they will be less likely to trip you up later.

15

Develop a section in your classroom for storing used curriculum. Ask a member to catalog this, and keep a card file by topic or scripture reference.

16

Delegate responsibilities and share the classroom workload. Ask a member or class officer to maintain the class roster and contact absentee members. Volunteers can assist with minor details such as straightening the classroom, moving chairs, and passing out hymnals. Ask your class officers to handle all duties not directly related to presenting the lesson.

17

Enjoy your class. Begin with a smile each Sunday morning. Spend time with the individuals in the class. Laugh and feel good about being Christians and learning together. Feeling at ease in the classroom will help you create an environment that stimulates intimate sharing.

18

Expect occasional setbacks. Don't be surprised if there are days when no one seems interested in the lesson, attendance is at an all-time low, or complaints flourish. On some days you will not feel up to teaching the class enthusiastically. Know that next week will be better, and focus on the hope we have in Christ to make all things new.

19

Practice good study habits. Try to review and study your curriculum at the same time each week. This may be as early as the Sunday night or even the weekend before the lesson is to be taught. Gather all the materials you will need including a Bible, pencils, paper, curriculum and other commentaries, and find a comfortable chair in a quiet room.

20

Read your lesson each day. Spend thirty minutes each morning or night reading your lesson plan and scriptures. This will keep the lesson fresh in your mind, and allow you to relate daily experiences to the Bible verses being studied.

21

Make plans for an annual class picnic. Depending on the climate, hold the picnic late in the evening on the church lawn or during the early morning at a nearby lake or park. Have several members plan the event and give everyone plenty of notice. Urge each member to bring a friend as you open your class to growth.

22

Actively reach out to all members. Personal caring provides "roots" for your class. While thoughts are important, it is the action, putting feet to faith, which really touches people's lives. Do this by regularly sending personal notes to those who are absent each week. If a class member is celebrating a birthday or anniversary, send a card or note acknowledging the event.

23

Attend worship regularly. Teachers should lead through example by attending congregational worship. Invite different members to sit with you each week, or consider sitting together as a class periodically.

24

Seek input from members. Ask class members to list the topics they would like to discuss in future lessons. Also, personally evaluate your weekly lessons to discover which topics really motivate your class discussion and involvement.

25

De-stress your life. Ongoing stress can result in constant muscle tension, increased blood pressure, rapid heartbeat, and an elevated state of arousal—it's as if we cannot get out of "passing gear" (as opposed to our normal pace or shifting downward). Eventually, living with tension, arousal, and tightness becomes the norm, and we find ourselves more vulnerable to illness. What is keeping you tense?

26

Avoid stumbling blocks. Watch for peculiar habits or traits which may hinder your delivery. Shaky hands, a quiver in your voice, or a glance at the floor all convey a message of insecurity in your teaching. Practice speaking in front of a mirror, or videotape yourself as you practice presenting the lesson.

27

Be an encourager. If members are reluctant to get involved in class discussions or activities, find ways to break down barriers so they feel comfortable. Ask other members to reach out to these people, as well.

28

Lean on prayer for consolation in your personal life. Spend at least ten minutes in prayer each morning, afternoon, and evening. Prayer continues that personal relationship with God that most of us long for, and helps to switch our bodies into a more calm, peaceful mood.

29

Identify spiritual formation. Challenge members this week to think about specific moments in their lives where Christ became real. Using a time line, suggest that each person draw symbolic pictures that depict these pinnacles in their faith journey. Ask them to bring these to class next week and share them with other members.

30

Talk about problems in your class with other teachers. Even if you can't identify the underlying cause of the problem, talking about your feelings may trigger insight about the root of the problem. Engaging in conversation with another teacher may help you see it in a positive light.

31

Involve class members in lesson discussions. Prepare open-ended questions that require the class members to express feelings, ideas, and creative thoughts. Reword any question that could be answered with a simple "yes" or "no" response. For example, ask, "How would you feel if that happened to you?" or "How would you react to this situation?" Help members take ownership of the lesson by becoming fully involved.

32

Set goals to increase membership. Challenge class members to increase attendance by 25 percent within the next six months. Identify strategies that will help in achieving your goal such as inviting friends, telephoning inactive members, or making personal home visits to potential new members.

33

Join hands during prayer. Touch is an important element in communicating caring to class members. The joining of hands symbolizes the unending circle of God's love in your church family.

34

Be a peacemaker. Jesus Christ was a peacemaker, not a peacekeeper. This often means speaking the truth in love and serving as a mediator between class members if there is conflict. In the midst of classroom dissension, do not hesitate to speak up for what you know to be true.

35

Getting to know yourself involves opening yourself up to God's will as you prepare the lesson each week. Prayer, quiet time, ongoing study, and meditation will help you find answers about the ways that God can use you. When you feel more comfortable and accepting of yourself, you will begin to take risks as you teach. You will begin to expose your personal feelings during class time and share your faith in God.

36

Be prompt on Sunday morning. Arriving early and beginning on time shows that you care. If you begin your lesson on time, people will make a point of arriving in time to hear the message. Tardiness lessens the impact of your teaching skills and abilities.

37

Invite others to share their faith. Encourage class members or guest speakers to teach the lesson periodically. Are missionaries living in your area who are available to share their experiences? Ask your pastor to suggest church members who might be willing to share their faith story.

38

Get to know your class members. Invite several to lunch after worship on Sunday. Allow them to talk about their lives and carefully listen to what they say. Become interested in their concerns, goals, and personal dreams.

39

Ask God for patience when dealing with difficult members. Know that God loves you and is aware of your concerns. Have confidence that God is moved by your prayers and patiently wait for the response.

40

Establish a prayer routine. It is vital for members to participate in the prayer experience. Many teachers find asking for God's guidance through prayer a helpful way of beginning a class. An opening prayer used to gather class members into a more worshipful frame of mind at the end of fellowship time offers a way of refocusing everyone on the lesson. This communication with God can often set the spiritual tone for the class session.

41

Follow through with good intentions. Using the cards in your recipe file box (#2), write down several good intentions that will touch the lives of your members. As you complete each intention, check the item off your list. Your list might look something like this:

____Call Susan after her surgery Tuesday

____Send a card to John

____Pray for Peter's son

____Order curriculum for Sharon and Dave

42

Celebrate special days. Plan a monthly party to celebrate all birthdays and anniversaries. Ask two members to provide a beverage and dessert. Another option is to recognize these members at your monthly class socials.

43

Create an inviting environment. Make sure there are enough chairs, Bibles, and hymnals for every member and visitor each week. Encourage members to allow visitors to be seated first.

44

Reach out to those in need. Spend a Sunday helping to feed the homeless at a local shelter. Afterward, discuss how as a class you can help meet some of the physical, emotional, and spiritual needs you learned about during your outing.

45

Make an effort to understand your lesson each week. Reread the lesson and Bible verses prior to Sunday morning. It is important to know all of the characters involved, their personalities, and their relationship with God in order to teach with personal conviction.

46

Laugh with your class. Remember, a cheerful heart does good! Laughter helps break down relationship barriers and enables you to feel intimately bonded.

47

Take spiritual risks. Faith is a dynamic, forward-looking relationship with our Creator. However, when we become too careful with our Christian faith, we can miss out on the real exhilaration of life—God's serendipities. Remember to stretch, venture out, and take risks as you put your ultimate trust in God.

48

Reach out to inactive members. Send personal notes to inactive members who have missed several weeks in a row. Follow up with a phone call and invite them back to Sunday school. If they are friends of active members, have the member call and extend an invitation back to Sunday school.

49

Go online to keep communication strong. Take advantage of the Internet to talk frequently with members through E-mail. Ask class members to share E-mail addresses with one another during fellowship time. The Internet is an inexpensive and fun way to keep in touch.

50

Get to know yourself. Identify your fears, dreams, doubts, and questions. Be honest with yourself so that you can relate honestly to your members. A teacher who is genuine risks sharing his life with others and creating an atmosphere of loving acceptance in the classroom.

51

Plan trips and outings outside the classroom. Check the newspaper for upcoming concerts, art shows, or other events that will appeal to your members. Then enjoy your leisure time together.

52

Create interest in your class. Use an innovative bulletin board right outside your classroom door with vibrant colors and creative titles to get the attention of those who walk by. Include on your board a listing of prayer concerns, the topics of the month's lessons, dates of class service projects and socials, and other pertinent information about your members.

53

Listen for God's answers. Often we become so involved in pouring out our troubles and woes that we forget to listen for answers. The Bible tells of God speaking in dreams, visions, and images. Jesus told of God dwelling "within." Encourage class members to keep a paper and pen handy during their daily prayer and devotional time. As they think of specific needs or answers to concerns, suggest that they write these insights down. Often these thoughts are direct answers to prayer and concerns.

54

Retire early on Saturday night. Have you ever been taught by someone who couldn't quite "get it together"? Perhaps he or she yawned the entire class time or was unprepared. Plenty of rest on Saturday night enables you to be more effective in offering teaching that changes lives. Plan to retire early this week so you can give your class your best.

55

Be in service to church members. There are many opportunities for your class to reach out in service to others. A few ideas include helping at church workdays, volunteering to babysit in the nursery during midweek events, writing letters for the sick, holding a fund-raiser to help with a church project, or mowing lawns for shut-ins. What ways can your class help on an ongoing basis?

56

Spruce up your classroom. Keep bulletin boards updated inside the room. Ask for someone to donate an area rug. Put colorful posters or pictures on the walls. These simple changes will help promote a feeling of the spiritual warmth of Christ.

57

Hold a food drive for those in crisis. Work with other classes to plan this drive. Publicize the drive churchwide, and celebrate God's bounty together.

58

Write about your spiritual pilgrimage. Do you remember the time you asked Jesus Christ to come into your life, or did you grow up knowing the Lord's love? How has God helped you through the trials in your life? Try to make your faith story come from the "eyes of your soul" this Sunday as you share it with class members. Use the time as a way of connecting with members so that they will want to seek the same fulfillment and blessings you have experienced.

59

Have patience. The challenge of Hebrews 12:1 is this: "Let us run with perseverance the race that is set before us." Perseverance involves not giving up in times of crisis, but "hanging in" until changes occur. Our Lord reminds us of the virtue of perseverance and asks us to wait upon him.

60

Learn from life's challenges. Life does not move on a level plain. For Jesus, after the mountaintop experience of his baptism came the valley with the temptation of Satan. Rather than letting these troubles drive a wedge between himself and God, Jesus chose to let it bring him closer to God.

61

Focus on love for one another. Have a candlelight potluck dinner, and ask members to bring their spouses or best friends. Provide transportation for those who need it.

62

Design a class web page on the Internet. Ask a computer whiz to design a class home page that can be updated regularly. Members and guests can access this page to read about upcoming events, topics of study, or class needs. If your church has a home page, find out how to link your class page to the church's web page.

63

Seek control today. Most of us feel helpless when things get out of our control. That is where faith comes in. Faith is the conviction that there is One who is in control, whose nature is love. When fatigue and desperation tell you, "Throw in the towel; give up," remember the words of the psalmist: "Take delight in the LORD, and he will give you the desires of your heart" (Psalm 37:4).

64

Be open to the power of the Holy Spirit. If you sense a need to pray, then pray. If you feel led to call a student on the phone, follow through. Appreciate this spontaneity as the Holy Spirit prompts you to share the love of God in the midst of a structured, harried day.

65

Share together. Consider starting a midweek sharing group with class members. This can provide an additional setting for personal growth and group interaction. Members can grow in spiritual understanding as well as in love for one another.

66

Expect miracles to happen. Prayer is communication with a living God, and answers should be expected. Bring an attitude of anticipation to your class this week as you pray together and share answers to prayers.

67

Join a volunteer organization. Contact an organization like Habitat for Humanity to see how your class can get involved in constructing homes or other helpful projects for people in need. Recruit members to commit to the project financially, prayerfully, or physically.

68

Ask for volunteers to assist with class growth. Recruit active members to visit absent class members as well as newcomers. Arrange a time when they can share what they learned from their visits. If the inactive member is having problems at home, share this information with your pastor.

69

Watch your teaching time. Use time segments to ensure that all lesson material is covered. Estimate what an appropriate time allotment should be for each segment of your class period, and work to stay within this. You might allow five minutes to greet members, take roll, and collect the offering. Another five minutes could be used for prayer requests and concerns. Next, spend five minutes preparing for the lesson by singing several hymns. In an hour-long class, you would have already used fifteen minutes. Spend the remaining forty-five minutes wisely as you lead your class in understanding the lesson and scriptures for the day.

70

Send a quarterly letter to the names on your roll, as well as to prospective members. Ask a member to write a brief synopsis of the upcoming lessons along with the scriptures that will be studied. Also, inform members of any changes in the class time and format, and list the dates and times of upcoming socials. Finally, include a list of the current class roster.

71

Organize an ongoing phone chain. Ask for volunteers to call people during the week prior to the Sunday lesson or special event. Sometimes a brief reminder is all it takes to activate those who have fallen into a slump with attendance.

72

Start Caring Circles. Divide your class into groups of three. Each Caring Circle will have one leader and two members. Let each circle know they are to pray for one another, get together periodically for lunch, and let the group leader know if they have special concerns or will be absent. The leader of each group will relay information about prayer concerns and absences to the teacher each week.

73

Capture your class on film. Videotape your class in action. Show the video at a family night supper. Allow time for personal testimonies of "What My Class Means to Me." Consider the ways your members can promote the benefits of Sunday school to others.

74

Work with the nursery staff to ensure that the area is clean and safe. If you have young parents in your class, the nursery facilities can help or hinder attendance each week. Ask for volunteers to help keep the nursery spotless by disinfecting the toys each week, changing the linens, providing a sign-in sheet, and finding qualified nursery workers.

75

Take advantage of the seasons. Holidays provide the perfect excuse to gather for celebration and fun. Class members can enjoy caroling at Christmastime, a Thanksgiving hayride, a St. Patrick's Day progressive dinner, or a May Day picnic. Whatever the occasion, use a seasonal theme to add to the festivities.

76

Create a group card for a member who is ill. Keep large pieces of construction paper or poster board in the classroom. Ask members to write a loving message and sign their names. Assign one member the task of delivering the card, along with the Sunday school lesson.

77

Do not stand in judgment. Avoid making judgments about any class member, especially one not strong in the Christian faith or in biblical teachings. Teachers are commissioned to teach God's Word so that faith can be the expected result.

78

Recruit help with transportation. Ask for volunteers who will provide transportation to Sunday school or other churchwide events. Publicize this outreach service so that all interested members and visitors know that it is available.

79

Use storytelling as a method of teaching. Remember how Jesus used parables to share God's message? Tell stories from your own life of how God was revealed to you. Ask members to consider doing the same in upcoming class sessions.

80

Start a class round-robin letter. Write a personal letter about your life to all class members. Attach it to the class roster. Send the letter to the name at the top of the roster list, asking her to attach news about her life. She, in turn, will send the letter to the next member on the roster, who will attach more information. When you receive the final copy of the round-robin letter, take it to Sunday school and post it on the bulletin board for all members to enjoy.

81

Decorate your classroom. Take advantage of garage sales to inexpensively furnish your class with shelves, chairs, or other furniture. Meet members for an early breakfast, then caravan to area garage sales. Spend time cleaning and refinishing the furniture as a way of getting to know one another.

82

Combine classes. Share a lesson with another adult class or even a youth or children's class. Invite everyone to participate in the discussion as a way of learning from the different ages involved.

83

Make a point today to respond reflectively to those around you. This does not mean that you have to agree with everyone, but this type of acceptance shows that you care. Use this means of communication during the Sunday school lesson this week, too.

84

Strengthen your teaching commitment. Jesus' ministry was one of making choices. As our Lord confronted people in different situations, he encouraged them to make decisions about their life—to choose between good and evil. Consider your commitment to teach, and pray that God will strengthen it.

85

Establish a class tradition. Traditions are important, especially in our transient, fast-paced society where the meaning of ritual and heritage is often diluted. Traditions offer a sense of identity in an impersonal era; they bond class members to one another, helping them to become rooted in the world. If you have no special class traditions, talk with members about creating some.

86

Review your knowledge of the Old Testament. Using Bible commentaries, spend time reviewing and studying the Old Testament. Discuss these scriptures with class members and talk about the differences between the Old and New Testaments.

87

Know the message of your material. Don't forget to read your Sunday school material today. You would be surprised at how many teachers just skim for the main idea. This may work for the "experts," but you need to know exactly what the author is saying, not just the general message being conveyed.

88

Pay attention to your commitments. Remember, Jethro advised Moses to "share the workload" as a way of protecting Moses and his people from stress and weariness. Are you taking on too many commitments that have increased your level of stress?

89

Let your faith in Christ shine. John the Baptist came to point us to the light which was in Jesus Christ. The light Jesus brings lets others know that we are children of God. Read John 1:5.

90

Pray for those around the world. Pray for families of all nationalities who have no food or clothing. Consider financially sponsoring someone in an undeveloped country through your local church missions. See if class members have interest in sponsoring this project.

91

Avoid attaching labels to your class members. A person who has been labeled as "carefree" in your class might try to live up to her name. Likewise, a meek person who is considered "shy and introverted" may never break out of his shell. Instead of looking at just one dominant trait of your class members, look at their personalities as a whole.

92

End your worry habit. Discuss worrying with class members. Offer ideas that prevent you from worrying such as keeping busy and praying about problems and concerns. Encourage members to involve themselves in the life of the church, as a busy mind has no time for worry.

93

Use small groups. Consider using small groups for class discussions if you rely heavily on lecture style teaching. Vary the groups each week so that newcomers can become acquainted with all class members.

94

Let God unify your class. The scripture "For where two or three are gathered together in my name, I am there among them" (Matthew 18:20) must become a reality for the entire class if you are to learn to lean on God for guidance, comfort, and strength.

95

Avoid letting one member dominate class discussions. Sometimes overly enthusiastic members jump at every opportunity to speak, yet this may intimidate more reserved members. Stay in control as the class leader and call on those who may be hesitant to speak out.

96

Check your teaching qualities. Effective characteristics of a Sunday school teacher include being genuine and honest, secure in faith and self-image, a good listener, positive and affirming, and fun to be around. These are all qualities that can be developed. Which ones do you need to nurture?

97

Take time out from teaching. If you are feeling burned out or have become too negative or critical of the members in your class, taking a few Sundays off might be excellent therapy. Jesus set a good example for us when he retreated to be alone with God. This time-out renewed his spirit and enabled him to live out his ministry. A week or two off from teaching can give a harried teacher time to reflect and recharge.

98

Try a role play this week. Role playing or a minidrama can be a fun and innovative teaching method for adults. Involve different members in the acting, then let the group analyze the scenario and plot the best outcome.

99

Lean on the gift of music. Music is a favorite learning tool, even in adult classes. If there are class members who play an instrument or enjoy singing, encourage them to lead the class singing before the lesson each week. Ask youth members in your church to come and teach contemporary Christian songs. Playing recorded music before class helps provide an environment that is warm and inviting.

100

Establish eye contact when you teach. Look at each class member as he or she enters the room, and continue to follow this pattern while you teach. Eye contact helps establish a one-to-one relationship with class members. This communication tool builds trust between you and your class members.

101

Greet your members and guests. Welcome class members and visitors as they arrive and call them by name. Use name tags if you have a large or new class. Remember, our names are just as special as our personalities.

102

Do a classroom check. Take time today to run by the church to see if your classroom is clean. Count the chairs to make sure that there are enough for all members and possible visitors. If you are unable to do this, ask a volunteer to help.

103

Become fit together. If your church has a softball or volleyball team, encourage members to join. If not, form your own class team. Plan a Sunday school picnic where you can play against other adult classes.

104

Build self-esteem among members. Nurture and affirmation are the necessary ingredients to encourage self-esteem. Let each person know he is appreciated. Encourage those who are not involved to take on more class responsibility and praise them for doing so.

105

Grow in faith. As Christians, we are challenged to grow in faith. In which areas do you need to grow (trust in God, love for others, patience, acceptance, hope)?

106

Get to know the visitors to your class. Have class members introduce their visitors during sharing time. Encourage all members to reach out during fellowship time, as well as after class, to greet these guests.

107

Relate the Bible to life. Relate your biblical lessons to happenings in the lives of your class members. Personal involvement and relational aspects of teaching provide effective ways to influence your class members with the gospel message.

108

Start at home with discipleship. Jesus' final emphasis in his ministry was to "go into all the world and make disciples...and teach." Jesus' commandment begins with our personal witness at home as we share our faith with family members and pray for a gracious and open dialogue.

109

Include your pastor in your class activities. Extend a special invitation to the pastor to attend a lesson or class social event. Ask your pastor to teach a lesson as a way of getting to know class members on a personal level.

110

Spend time alone for renewal. Remember that the Bible admonishes us: "Be still, and know that I am God!" (Psalm 46:10). Make plans to use this alone time to seek an unending source of strength, renewal, and encouragement as you follow the example of our Lord.

111

Create an awareness for missions. Set up a mission corner in your room, and display a map with flags pinned on locations where your church is in service to others. Ask members to correspond with sponsored missionaries, and consider making pledges to help them with their work.

112

Remember that God loves you. If you are going through a personal slump, remember that God is there. God feels our pain and sorrow, and as difficult as life may seem, has a definite plan for each of us. Continue to ask for God's blessings in your life, and live with this hope.

113

Do random acts of kindness. These acts of kindness are as common as a cold and can be caught just as easily. Consider calling a class member who has stopped attending, or writing a thank-you note to someone who contributed to the lesson last week.

114

Incorporate communion in class worship. Ask your pastor to hold a communion service after the lesson this week. Breaking the bread together is not only symbolic of the life Christ gave us, but it can bridge any communication gaps your members may have.

115

Plan an ecumenical gathering. Make plans to join with a Sunday school class from another church, denomination, or religion. You might call a nearby Catholic church or Jewish synagogue and set up a joint fellowship time with an adult class. Talk openly about your similarities and differences and share your love for one another as children of God.

116

Discuss setting short- and long-term goals. Make sure you discuss goals with your officers and members periodically. Your goals might include increasing attendance, strengthening outreach, or supporting local missions. Write these down and evaluate them periodically.

117

Work on your self-control. Read Galatians 5:22-23: "The fruit of the Spirit is love, joy, peace, patience, kindness, generosity, faithfulness, gentleness, and self-control." Which of these "fruit" do you need to work on?

118

Lean on the little things to strengthen the whole. How can you touch the lives in your class through small gestures? Some suggestions include making a phone call just because you care, meeting members for dinner after work, sending thank-you cards for participating in class, or bringing homemade muffins to share on Sunday.

119

Take a time-out to reflect on your Christian journey. Use your time-out to view a brilliant sunrise or sunset, enjoy a panoramic view of nature on a hike, or watch birds feed in your backyard. Thank God for this special time, and celebrate the gift of nature.

120

Share agape love. This self-giving love is filled with compassion and empathy and seeks what is best for others. Agape love continues to show compassion even when a person acts unloving.

121

Thank others. Thank God for Sunday school teachers who have touched your life in the past. Write these people letters, thanking them for personal affirmation and training during earlier years. Encourage class members to do the same.

122

Reach out with class socials. Plan social events where class members bring unchurched visitors. Include creative crowd breakers so newcomers can get involved. Follow up with a personal phone call inviting visitors to Sunday school, and ask members to bring them to their first class visit.

123

Watch your attitude when teaching. Leave personal problems and negative attitudes at home. Begin your lesson with prayer, and ask God to lead you in touching lives with the selfless love of Christ.

124

Understand and appreciate the hidden grace of God. Deep within each of us are reservoirs of peace, strength, and assurance. We usually know nothing about these until we are forced to call upon them and use them. Know that the grace of God is present in abundance far beyond what we dare to expect or can imagine.

125

Choose Prayer Partners this week. Select names during class and suggest that these be kept a secret. Encourage members to pray for the person they chose, then to follow up with a special deed—a note in the mail or fresh flowers on their doorstep.

126

Plan a class retreat. Not only are retreats important for spiritual renewal, they are fun for fellowship and personal growth. When planning your retreat, allow ample time for education, fellowship, recreation, service, worship, and rededication.

127

Radiate enthusiasm. Your teaching expectations, attitude, and reactions can determine the response of your students. If you're excited about the gospel message, you will radiate joy. Students will want to be near you and learn from you.

128

Watch the tone of your voice. Instead of communicating in anger and harshness, speak in a manner that is nonthreatening. Words have the power to lift someone up or tear someone down, depending on how they are used.

129

Really listen to class members. Take the time during the week to touch base with several class members. Talk about their interests and listen as they share! Find out what bothers them, what they dream about, what they fear. Remember, you are influencing each member's spiritual life.

130

Be creative. Members will respond to a lesson if you use creative teaching aids or props to stimulate discussion. Use biblical costumes to strengthen a character's image, background music during a story, or pictures and maps to describe the topographical area where your lesson takes place.

131

Risk being open. As you risk being open and talk about your life struggles as a Christian, members will see that you are accessible as a friend and teacher. They will learn to trust you and feel comfortable enough to express their feelings within the confines of your class.

132

Teach for a response. Prepare your lessons so visitors will feel compelled to return. If you have new visitors and your class is in the middle of an ongoing discussion from a previous lesson, review the topic so they too can participate.

133

Examine your words. While the world is lacking in positive role models, your words have a tremendous influence on the lives of those around you. Thoughts, feelings, and behavior mirror the soul, but your spoken word has the profound ability to build up or tear down anyone in its path.

134

Stay rested. In order to teach and care for your class effectively we must get adequate restful sleep. We are a tired generation, trying to burn the candle at both ends. But in the midst of wanting to get the most out of every day, we forget that we are human with human needs. Getting restful sleep is important to feel recharged and healthy.

135

Incorporate Prayer Partners in your class. Take a Polaroid picture of each class member. Tape the person's name at the bottom of the photo along with phone number and address. Put all the pictures in a box, face down, and have each member select one. When everyone has a photo of someone else, ask each one to take the picture home, tape it to the dresser mirror, and pray for this person during the upcoming week. Bring the pictures back each Sunday, and choose new Prayer Partners.

136

Talk about thankfulness. Tape a piece of paper on the class bulletin board, and at the top write the words "For This I Am Grateful." During fellowship time, ask class members to write down anything they are thankful for— healing, friends, family, special talents, answers to prayer, and more.

137

Encourage church membership. Has everyone in your class committed to becoming a member of the church? Church membership can help people concretize their personal identity as they participate in worship, programs, committees, choirs, and outreach programs, along with Sunday school. This leadership commitment affords all a way to thank God for their talents while touching others' lives in Jesus' name.

138

Seek inner healing. Paul said, "I can do all things through Christ, who strengthens me." Jesus knew this as he retreated to the wilderness and to the mountain to pray for strength. Go to the depths of your soul for that secret place of the most high God where you can find creative and healing solitude.

139

Name spiritual experiences. Ask members, "What did you think today that was of God?" Some examples might be loving thoughts, empathetic thoughts, thoughts of passion, or benevolent thoughts.

140

Practice give-and-take during discussions. This offers each person a chance to speak, offer personal viewpoints, and learn to stand up for his or her beliefs in a safe environment. Let your class be a loving testing ground where Christians can grow.

141

Revitalize your personal faith. Renew your commitment to spend time each day in solitude. You might do this at a time that allows you to get outdoors in the early morning or late afternoon. Post this schedule, and check off the days you follow through as you marvel at being one with our Lord.

142

Be persistent. If you have inactive members who show little interest in reconnecting, continue to call and invite them to class. Paul offers strength for being steadfast in Acts 2:42: "They devoted themselves to the apostles' teaching and fellowship, to the breaking of bread and the prayers." Persistence involves loyalty to the member's potential instead of what you might experience at a negative moment.

143

Act on impulse with good deeds. The Bible teaches us that "faith without works is also dead" (James 2:26). When you feel a nudge to call a lonely member, do a home visit, or even provide a meal to someone who is experiencing problems, do it now! The longer you wait between the mere thought and the actual deed, the more likely you are to procrastinate.

144

Tape your class singing. Homebound members enjoy hearing tapes of class members singing favorite hymns. Consider delivering the tapes one Sunday morning as a class instead of having a lesson.

145

Encourage members to keep a journal. This personal diary can help members get organized for spiritual growth as they document feelings and thoughts each day. As they read their journal several weeks later, they will see their faith at its highs and lows, peaks and valleys. The journal can also become an intimate place where members can ventilate, contemplate, problem-solve, and dream—without feeling threatened or intimidated.

146

Reevaluate your goals for growth. Goals help to turn hopes and dreams into purpose and reality. Without specific goals, you have no guidelines by which to measure growth. Setting classroom goals will help you when attendance declines and enthusiasm subsides.

147

Stay updated. Keep a calendar on the wall in your classroom. Write in the lesson topics to be studied for the upcoming month. Also, circle the birthdays or anniversaries of members. Be sure to draw attention to the upcoming dates each week.

148

Celebrate class worship. Set up a makeshift altar in the classroom with an open Bible. Have a journal and pen available for members to record prayer requests. Refer to this altar during your prayer time, and read requests each Sunday from the updated journal.

149

Make Christlike behavior your aim. Actions speak louder than words. Let your daily actions exemplify the Christian faith as you stand up for a friend, refuse to participate in gossip, and forgive someone who has hurt you.

150

Encourage personal sharing. Your class is a support group for your members—a place where they can feel free to express concerns, needs, and problems in their lives. Alert your pastor to a member who is undergoing personal or health problems and is in need of counseling.

151

Don't hold a grudge. Clinging to a grudge is counterproductive. It keeps us from dealing with the problem that initially led us to hold the grudge, and resentment breeds discontent. Openly resolve disagreements.

152

Realize that change is inevitable. Remind members that the one thing that never changes is Jesus Christ: he is the same yesterday, today, and tomorrow. Knowing that faith in God is secure will help your members deal with problems of change through reasonable decisions and choices.

153

Write press releases. If you are having a special event in your classroom or your class is participating in a service project, inform the neighborhood or local newspaper so they can report the information. Always provide pertinent class information to your church office for newsletters and bulletins, too.

154

Stay enthusiastic each week. Enthusiasm means "filled with God." Whether you have one class member or many, continue teaching your lesson with enthusiasm each week.

155

Hug your class members. Touch is critical in communicating genuine care and concern to the students in the Sunday school class. A pat on the shoulder, a hug, a firm handshake, or other physical strokes often generate a stronger sense of caring and concern than spoken words. The warmth of the human touch can erase even the most uncomfortable situations and struggles.

156

Continue to set aside quiet time. Use this time to reflect on the past week and sort through the busyness of your schedule. Let this time be a source of spiritual strength as you communicate with God, read scriptures for inspiration, and listen to God's voice in response.

157

Stay rooted in the world through personal caring. This will give added meaning to your life. Remember, while thoughts are important, it is the action—putting feet to our Christian faith—that really touches lives.

158

Acknowledge the gifts of others. Realize that each person in your class is his own person with unique ideas, abilities, and gifts. Thank God daily for each student's individuality.

159

Take care of your own needs. Remember that you are a person first and a teacher second. We cheat class members if we ignore our own needs. If we are full of tensions and anxieties, perhaps we are not loving ourselves enough. Unless we care for ourselves, we may not be adequate to love and care for our class.

160

Take advantage of modern communication. If you can't visit someone in person to let her know you care, the telephone places a close second in showing concern for others. Keep the conversation focused on the other person. Spend time listening while on the telephone; you may pick up clues about the other person that could alert you to important dates, events, or even problems she is having in her life.

161

Always show forgiveness. We all make mistakes in our lives; no one is immune from this. The Sunday school teacher who offers unconditional forgiveness constantly moves into a closer relationship with class members. Forgiveness is the whole essence of the gospel. And this forgiveness should be a part of our caring relationship with the students in our class.

162

Stay on a firm schedule. It is easy to stay in lengthy discussions about an upcoming social or have one member dominate the prayer requests for minutes on end. Although these concerns are important, it is also important to remember that students come to class to learn the Word of God. It is your job to manage the group so that this learning can take place.

163

Be innovative. Could a short-term study give additional insight into Christian living? Would a new method of teaching help to involve more members in the learning process? Perhaps changing the seating to a circle or purchasing comfortable couches would help increase conversational levels and togetherness.

164

Follow Christ. Emphasize to members that Jesus came to teach us how to live and love. He taught us what God is like. Challenge them to share this love with others in the upcoming week.

165

Form a Care Team. This is a group of class volunteers who work specifically on class growth through letter writing, visitation, regular phone calls, and bringing visitors to class. Meet with this team regularly to address ways you can reach out to inactive members.

166

Study scriptures diligently. The Bible offers inspiration, strength, knowledge, and insight into human living. It will give you and your members fresh understanding about life and strength to proclaim Christ as Lord.

167

Watch your posture. Practice standing up straight when presenting the lesson. Studies show that posture is closely linked to the mood of the moment. If you are stiff and rigid, members may feel uncomfortable while speaking. If you are too loose and relaxed, members may become so relaxed that they lose their focus on the message being taught.

168

Avoid having favorites in class. Show concern for all members. As teachers, we must indelibly stamp the people in our classrooms with God's love. Our concern must be so intimate, so full of selfless love that each member knows we are authentic.

169

Set the stage. Be sure to plan ahead for Sunday morning by arriving early and making sure the room is ready for the lesson. Arrive at least fifteen minutes before class time so you can greet early arrivals personally. Make sure the chairs are straight, hymnals and Bibles are available, and the worship center is organized. Consider playing Christian music as members arrive.

170

Be approachable. Help class members accept their occasional feelings of discomfort by being genuine. Let them know that you too have experienced life's rocky paths and relate how your faith sustained you. Allow them the privilege of knowing that with God's help, they can weather any storm.

171

Hear God all day long. God speaks to us when we drive in rush-hour traffic, when a neighbor drops in unexpectedly for coffee, or when a child brings us a bouquet of colorful weeds from the backyard and says, "I love you."

172

Develop a relationship with each member. Make sure you discover each person's special interests, abilities, and needs. What are ways you can allow each member to use his talent in the classroom?

173

Be prepared. Keep on hand a supply of birthday, anniversary, thank-you, and sympathy cards, as well as stamps, so you can send cards to class members when appropriate. This provides you with the necessary ingredients to show that you care when the opportunity arises.

174

Lean on prayer when conflicts occur. Prayer can change things. If you find that relationships are strained in the classroom, continue to pray for those involved. Prayer can help unite the members and provide direction for problem-solving. Find strength in Psalm 55:17: "Evening and morning and at noon I utter my complaint and moan, and he will hear my voice."

175

Examine your priorities. Focus on what is most important in life. Jesus spoke of the need to count the cost before taking on anything new (Luke 14:28-33). The biblical passage in Matthew 5:37 instructs us to let our yes be yes and our no be no.

176

Enjoy downtime. Take time this afternoon to enjoy a cool drink and time alone. Sit outside and take in the beauty around you with all your senses—the sights, smells, colors. Meditate on favorite scriptures found in Psalms, and thank God for this special time.

177

Set aside a Caring Time each day. This may be after lunch or in the evening. Use this time to phone a member, write a short note, or plan upcoming celebrations of birthdays. Find the right Caring Time for you and make it a priority.

178

Talk about tithing. Christian stewardship is a way of life, and Jesus is the perfect example for us to follow. Jesus used every moment of his life to glorify God; we must do the same. Encourage members to make it a habit as they give 10 percent to the Sunday school and general church fund. Remind members that "God loves a cheerful giver" (2 Corinthians 9:7).

179

Glorify Christ with open communication. Talk with members after class and carefully listen to their responses. Are their lives being changed? Are they having difficulty relating biblical messages to their personal lives? Communicating regularly will help you create a style of teaching that will meet them where they are in life.

180

Come with expectation. The song "Something Good Is Going to Happen to You" fills many hearts with hope and anticipation. You can bring this same expectation and excitement to your classroom as you look for the small miracles that occur each day.

181

Be mindful of members who are absent. Make contact with absentees through personal phone calls or letters. A teacher's work does not end on Sunday morning; rather the job entails providing ongoing care throughout the week.

182

Experience grace. Nurture members in a warm classroom environment where grace can be experienced and faith in God will be the expected result. Remember, you may be the best Christian your class members know.

183

Take time for reflection. Do you remember a Christian who had a tremendous influence on your life? This is someone who made you feel loved, who made you want to learn what they knew, and who brought out the best in you. Did this special person believe in you? Affirm you? Encourage you? Consider how you can be this influential Christian in the lives of your members this week.

184

Reduce your teaching stress. Realize that you don't have to know all the answers. Sometimes it is embarrassing not to have a correct response to a member's question. Yet admitting that you don't know is one way of letting members know that you are real and approachable and are traveling on your own spiritual journey.

185

Guide your members. Help members find answers to faith questions by directing them to various resources: the pastors, the Director of Christian Education, the church or public library, another adult leader or teacher, or a specialist in a particular field.

186

Listen to the language of emotions. When feelings and thoughts are poured out and real listening occurs, your members feel affirmed and understood. Jesus exhibited listening skills as he patiently dealt with people and problems each day. Remember, in John 8:1-11, how Jesus patiently listened to the scribes and Pharisees as they accused the woman of adultery, his kind words to her, and how he solved the problem without harsh punishment? Other similar events share the same gospel message: Jesus listened intently to the problem before responding in love.

187

Interpret the language of behavior. Inappropriate laughter or comments, sudden tears, or a burst of temper have meaning just as words do. Try to look beyond the action to the underlying meaning of the behavior.

188

Build on individual strengths. Encourage class members to realize their full potential, and help them build on their strengths. Give all members a chance to shine in a special way, whether it is through group activities, personal caring, evangelism, leading group singing, baking cakes, or praying for others, so they can establish a higher sense of self. Let them know that God made each of us and that we complement one another.

189

Express feelings. Help members express their feelings this week without fear of being ridiculed. This can happen if you lead the way by interjecting your personal history into the lesson. Tell of faith struggles you have had. Share how God helped you cope with crises or disappointments and mention how you felt—afraid, nervous, empty. Your openness will encourage others to express themselves too.

190

Celebrate life! Make time during class to have fun; this adds the sparkle needed to break down barriers. A fun time may be during your opening announcements as members tell humorous stories, or you may plan a fun crowd breaker from time to time so members can enjoy one another.

191

Be genuine. The teacher is 90 percent of the teaching/learning equation. People do not follow ideas, they follow people. How can you attract others to your class with a genuine and winsome manner?

192

Seek completeness in all of life. Spiritual unrest or the search for inner peace is an unconscious motivator to seek completeness in life. Viktor Frankl has pointed out that this emotional unrest or inner tension is an indispensable prerequisite of mental health. When we experience inner tension we become motivated not to settle for physical comforts but to seek a more whole and complete condition. What changes would have to take place in your life for you to feel complete? How difficult would it be to implement these changes?

193

Touch lives with God's love. Come prepared this week to touch the lives of your members with the gospel message. Allow time to pray and meditate about the lesson and class members' needs. Again, arrive at the classroom at least fifteen minutes before starting time so you can collect your thoughts, pray, and relax before teaching begins.

194

Teach for learning to happen. Response is the key to teaching, and response takes time. Without it, however, you will never know if learning has taken place. Are members responding to the challenge of living as Christians today? If not, how can you change your method of teaching so God's grace is shared and faith in Jesus Christ is the result?

195

Make changes in the lesson format if needed. Listen to class members. Be sure you really hear your members' reactions to the Scriptures, their interpretations of the lessons, and their interaction in the classroom. Use this insight to make changes in the way the lesson is presented.

196

Be an example for members. Talk with members this week about your personal faith. Think of yourself as a stationary planet with many satellites revolving around you. Do your students see you as an example to follow?

197

Arrive at the church early on Sunday. Invite members to pray with you in the sanctuary before class time. Talk about your personal doubts and stumbling blocks and how God gives you strength to get through these times. Join hands, and pray together.

198

Plan quarterly class meetings and hold them in someone's home. These are great times to air grievances, take responsibility for actions, and list areas that need work. Make sure the time is publicized ahead of time so all members can attend. Share a favorite dessert afterward.

199

Lean on love. Read Matthew 11:28-30. Are you equipped to bear the burdens and failures of each class member? Lift up to God the troubles class members carry each day.

200

Schedule a work day at the church this month. Write the needed tasks on three-by-five-inch file cards. Let each member who attends choose a card and a task to complete; then enjoy a meal together at a favorite restaurant.

201

Realize that Christ nourishes us through one another. Take a moment before the lesson this Sunday to share your innermost thoughts. Read Psalm 31 together and talk about Christ as the Rock in your life. How can you help members feel more confident? Make a commitment to be more attentive to each member.

202

Remember to exercise. Exercise improves your mood and lowers stress. In fact, aerobic activity can reduce anxiety, tension, and stress while at the same time promoting clear thinking. Even exercising as little as twenty minutes, three times a week, appears to lower stress levels.

203

Spend time in prayer and quiet contemplation. Research shows that prayer produces alpha waves in the brain that are consistent with serenity and happiness. Prayer provides nourishment for your soul and helps refocus your attention on God's plan for your life.

204

Use group discussion as a teaching tool with a small class. Make sure this is an active conversation that includes all members present. Ask everyone to come prepared by reading the scriptures and curriculum ahead of time. Challenge members to bring written questions to class, then work together in the group to solve a problem or arrive at a conclusion.

205

Spend time in solitude. The gospel provides a wealth of insight into the need to be alone. Being alone, as seen in the life of Jesus, need not be a time for feeling lonely, for we can feel lonely in the midst of a crowd. Being alone can be a time for finding meaning in one's life. Find time today for inner healing as you take time to nurture yourself.

206

Change your class meeting location. On a clear day, take the chairs outside and teach under a large shade tree. Enjoy the wonderment of nature as you teach the lesson. Remember to list changes in your class's format in the church bulletin or newsletter.

207

Realize that actions speak much louder than words. While it is important to say the words "I care about you," it is also important to show this love. Do this by taking a meal or organizing a work team to assist with housekeeping for a member who is ill.

208

Find creative ways to use each member's talent. Seek to discover each person's God-given talent whether it is academic, athletic, social, spiritual, or something else. Talk about the scripture found in Matthew 25:15: "To one he gave five talents, to another two, to another one, to each according to his ability."

209

Believe in forgiveness. Openly say the words "I'm sorry" if there is conflict between you and another member. The best way to admit that you were wrong is to be genuine and honest. Encourage members to share their feelings. Talk about how much God has forgiven us and how we are to also forgive others. (Read Matthew 18:21-34 together.)

210

Celebrate spiritual formation. Ask class members to think about their spiritual journey and identify turning points where God was made real. Allow for personal sharing during class.

211

Enjoy your members. Some of us lose that free spirit as we grow older. However, making time during the week to have fellowship with members will enhance your relationships. Your fun times might be spur-of-the-moment events—like an early breakfast at a nearby restaurant before work or impromptu picnics in the church garden.

212

Volunteer today. Encourage class members to volunteer in church activities such as Vacation Bible School, youth programs, or family activities. For inspiration, read Isaiah 6:8.

213

Glorify God. Take an early morning hike and enjoy the beauty of God's world—the flowers, trees, sky, and people. Remember that stewardship involves responsible spending and includes using our time, talents, body, and mind to glorify God. Read Matthew 25:14-30.

214

Think about your Christian values. The cost of being a Christian in a secular world is high, but God demands unconditional surrender to his will. He asks us to do things that take a great deal of effort and that may be painful. Especially when we are faced with conflicting values, it is important to know that standing strong is what Christians are to do even though it is not easy at the moment.

215

Celebrate your past. Pull out your childhood photos and enjoy them with several members. Talk about your interests during childhood, as well as your dreams and fears. What were your favorite foods, television shows, games, and activities? Ask class members to bring their childhood photos and post them on a bulletin board.

216

Pray without ceasing. Spontaneous prayers throughout the day can help you recognize the love of God in your life. A simple song can sometimes be a powerful prayer. So can a poem or scripture that describes feelings about a specific topic. Or a one-sentence "thank you, God" can be said at any time.

217

Do an attitude check today. Take steps to break the habit of soothing spiritual unrest with emotional outbursts by using the following principles:

Never allow yourself to get too <u>h</u>arried.

Never allow yourself to get too <u>a</u>ngry.

Never allow yourself to get too <u>b</u>ored.

Never allow yourself to get too <u>i</u>ntense (or stressed).

Never allow yourself to get too <u>t</u>ired.

218

Acknowledge Jesus Christ as Lord and Savior. For many people, spirituality and a belief in God through Jesus Christ have been abstract concepts rather than present realities. Intellectually, we say that we believe, but this reality has not had much bearing on how we treat ourselves or others. Therefore, nothing we do in life is more important than our spiritual growth as we acknowledge Jesus Christ as our Lord and personal Savior.

219

Live each day to the fullest. Look for the hope and beauty of our Christian faith in those around you. This involves taking time to appreciate God's world instead of hurrying throughout the day. Meditate on the scripture found in Philippians 4:8: "Whatever is true, . . . think about these things."

220

Sing hymns together. Ask your church to provide hymnals for your class, or have a fund-raiser to purchase them. Before you sing the words to the hymns, talk about them with members. Explain denominational traditions and liturgies, then sing favorite songs together.

221

Involve all members in class discussions. When asking questions, consider going in a circle. This will encourage everyone to share something regarding the lesson instead of relying on the same people.

222

Check your communication. Healthy communication in the classroom involves a transformation in thinking, from wishing others were like us to being so accustomed to their idiosyncrasies and special quirks that we wonder how we ever got along without them. When we compassionately communicate "I love you unconditionally," God will strengthen our Sunday school class.

223

Love yourself. Remember that you are a person first. We cheat our families and our class members if we ignore our own needs. We have been given the Great Commandment in the Gospels, "You shall love your neighbor as yourself" (Mark 12:31). This verse presupposes that we love ourselves. If you are full of personal tensions and anxieties, try to love yourself more.

224

Grow from the inside out. When we acknowledge our inner spirit, our soul, we begin to embrace the true character of our being—the very essence of who we are. Only then are we able to tackle life's demands with greater enthusiasm. Spiritual fulfillment has always been available for everyone, but we must allow this realization to become a vital part of our life today. As teachers we must enthusiastically teach our members about spiritual wholeness.

225

Instruct those who visit in the homes of class members. Help volunteers realize that each visit will be different. Suggest taking along a copy of the class curriculum, newsletter, and pamphlet about your church's activities to share with the person. Volunteers should stay just a few minutes on the first visit and be sensitive to other persons' needs.

226

Spirituality prepares us for eternity. Spiritual strength will help us resist moral weakness, and provide protection during times of personal crises. But we need to strengthen our spiritual lives for a third reason—as preparation for an eternity in the presence of God. The principle of life remains sound: everything external deteriorates and decays. Only that which we are on the inside remains. All of us know it is so.

227

Pause for spiritual reflection. Spend time outdoors today. Think about the colors, textures, and scents of God's creation. Make cloud pictures and reflect on other days when you found inner peace and tranquility in God's outdoor kingdom.

228

Talk about conversational prayer this week. Tell members that talking to God aloud is like talking to a very dear friend. He is all-caring and wants to know our innermost thoughts, fears, and dreams. We don't have to use impressive words to get God's attention; sincere words are much more important. Ask members to offer conversational prayers at the end of worship time.

229

Keep duplicate records for convenience. Maintain accurate records of all your members and visitors, including names, addresses, home and work phone numbers. Duplicate these records so you have access to them both at church and at home. Consider providing each member with a listing of names and phone numbers of the entire class.

230

Allow imperfection. One of the biggest stumbling blocks for teachers is that they often develop unrealistic expectations of themselves and their class members. These expectations can become self-defeating when events and persons outside of your control thwart your attempts at perfection. By realizing that you are human and imperfect, you become more tolerant of the imperfection in class members.

231

Laugh aloud. Laughter helps you relax and let go of worries. Most people will admit that taking time for a light moment, especially when they are worried or stressed, helps alleviate some of the tension in the body.

232

Reclaim the time in your life. Is your life cluttered with too many activities? Being involved in too many activities may cause suffering for your loved ones as well as for yourself, but God can help. Freedom from the stress and anxieties of a hurried life can happen when we move beyond self and turn humbly to our Lord for guidance.

233

Talk about witnessing. Ask, "Is it easy or difficult to be a Christian witness?" Is it possible for members to gain the strength, knowledge, and courage to share their faith in God when peers or co-workers often tear down their very belief? What situations do your members face that are difficult? Remind them of God's everlasting strength in the midst of trying situations.

234

Seek calm amidst the storms. Every teacher experiences difficulties from time to time—angry members who drop out, attendance or discussion lulls, or terminal exhaustion. Real faith begins when we are stripped of any human wisdom and pride. We fall to our knees and pray "Lord, you know my needs. I am a teacher." And with that he smiles and says, "Peace, be still." The winds cease, and there is calm.

235

Focus on quiet time. The Bible offers inspiration, knowledge, and insight into human living and can offer a strong background to every Christian who is striving for a deeper faith. Take a Sunday to share favorite Bible verses with members, and ask them to do the same. Discuss the importance of turning to God's Word for knowledge and strength.

236

Involve new members. Gently guide new members into leadership positions according to their spiritual gifts and talents. These newcomers have the greatest potential for evangelism, since their friends and acquaintances may be unchurched persons or new Christians.

237

Name spiritual experiences. Encourage members to get in the habit of naming daily spiritual experiences. Ask, "What did you do this week that was of God?" Some examples might include helping a friend, volunteering, comforting a co-worker or listening to a child.

238

Seek social support. Studies show that those who have strong social support systems are healthier and handle stress more effectively. If you need someone to talk to, consider joining a support group at your church or in your community.

239

Give to those in need. Ask members to clean out closets and collect unwanted clothing, small appliances, furniture, or toys for local organizations. Talk about the calling of Christians to care for those in need.

240

Reexamine your internal life. Each day God gives us opportunities to reexamine our life's direction and purpose. Life is full of these kinds of opportunities that, in the normal course of events, introduce a sobering wake-up call to us, regardless of how we may be living. What changes do you need to make as you deepen your personal relationship with God through Jesus Christ?

241

Love unlovely members. Finding good qualities in a member who is difficult is trying, even for the most patient teacher. Yet we have the commandment from Jesus to care especially for the unlovely, to reach out in compassion to those in need. Jesus tells us that "just as you did it to one of the least of these who are members of my family, you did it to me" (Matthew 25:40). Reach out with acceptance and unconditional love this week and watch how relationships change.

242

Set personal goals. What is it that you would like to achieve? Where are you headed with your career? With your spiritual life? How is your physical health? Whatever goals you feel are necessary, make a list of them and write two ways to take action so the goal will become a reality.

243

Make time for God. Becoming a Christian and learning to live in a Christlike manner are two completely different matters. Remind members this week that to learn about God through Jesus Christ and to grow spiritually we must make time every day for spiritual disciplines, including Bible study, prayer, meditation, and personal reflection.

244

Watch out for temptation. C. S. Lewis reminded us that only good people are bothered by temptation. Bad people don't consider it temptation because they always succumb to it! It is in these moments of temptation that we must encourage members to stand firm and deal with the opposition head-on by saying "no" or confronting the person.

245

Talk about personal attributes. Ask members to tell of specific attributes they need to have more confidence in sharing their faith. These may include honesty, openness, caring, listening, action, strength, courage, and risking. Challenge members to use these attributes as they tell someone of their love for Jesus this week.

246

Look directly at the member who is speaking. While listening, refuse to talk or even glance at anyone else in the classroom, even if just to smile. Each time you look away while listening to someone, your connection to that person is broken. Each time you pay attention, you show courtesy and respect.

247

Check your calendar today. What special dates or appointments are coming up? Write down the names of members celebrating birthdays or anniversaries this week. What about family members, friends, or neighbors? Have stamps and cards nearby to make caring convenient.

248

Offer a nonverbal witness. Have members list nonverbal ways they can let others know they are Christians. Examples such as giving a hug to someone who is hurting or doing a kind deed can be listed. Encourage members to follow through with this witness during the week.

249

Reflect and grow. Periodically allow time for reflection. Are class members involved in the lesson? Are they getting to know one another better? Is attendance steady and strong? Reflection will enable you and class leaders to make changes if you notice a lull in interest, involvement, or attendance.

250

Enjoy God's unique plan. Go on a walk today and pick a variety of wildflowers. Use them to make a flower arrangement for your class. Talk about how the flowers are all different, just as we are, and how God made each of us unique. Read together Ecclesiastes 3:11.

251

Embrace life. Have you ever taken time to follow a child around while playing? Children laugh, sing, climb, run, skip, and embrace life to the fullest as they engage in active play. For many adults, leisure time is spent lying on the couch or snoozing in bed. But activity and exercise can help inoculate us against stress and its effects.

252

Explore love. What does love mean? Even when you do all the right things, sometimes love is painful and disappointing. Always being loving is often easier said than done. Talk with your class about agape or selfless love. This kind of love that Jesus taught gives without regard to receiving anything in return.

253

Make a difference with your faith. Is your relationship with Jesus Christ making a difference in your attitude toward others? In your tolerance level with class members? In your outlook on life? In your priorities? In your involvement in the church? In your personal witness? Make changes today to ensure that you are Christlike in attitude.

254

Share the love of God. Watch for signs in members this week to see if someone seems saddened or preoccupied with personal problems. Be a witness for our Lord and share his love and assurance.

255

Change teaching methods this month. If your class is large enough, break into informal, small group discussions after an abbreviated class lecture. Challenge members to risk being open with others in the small group. Gather at the end of the period to discuss results of the discussion. Are members learning to relate the message of the Bible lesson to their personal lives?

256

Encourage members to cultivate an active prayer life. Suggest that they pray spontaneously throughout the day as they recognize the love of God in their lives. Verbally acknowledging the beauty of a sunrise, the opening bud on the rosebush, or the first raindrop on a cloudy day can enhance each member's relationship with God.

257

Telephone class members who are ill. During Sunday school hour, use a portable phone to call shut-ins. Let different members talk with the shut-in, then offer a prayer with that person.

258

Become sensitive to all class members. Realizing that criticism is painful, use this knowledge to become more caring in class interactions. Let the scripture in John 8:7—"Let anyone among you who is without sin be the first to throw a stone"—be your guide.

259

Meet the needs of class members. If attendance is down during a specific season, try to meet at an earlier time. This will leave more free time for those who want to spend afternoons recreating with friends and family. Some adult classes take advantage of the smaller numbers during the summer and meet in the church kitchen while taking turns preparing a light breakfast before the lesson.

260

Affirm accomplishments and special celebrations. A handwritten banner across the blackboard, a colorful balloon tied to someone's chair, or a "holy clapping of hands" are all ways to affirm someone. Whether a birthday, anniversary, job promotion, birth of a baby, or recovery from an illness, seek ways to celebrate victories of all members.

261

Make love your aim. Reach out in love to those you are in contact with—your family members, coworkers, friends and neighbors, and church family. In everything you do or say, make the decision to love another person as Christ has loved you—unconditionally and always thinking of others.

262

See the rainbow. Is a class member facing disappointment? Sometimes when it rains, it pours. When those we love face disappointment, it can seem as if the rain is unending. Yet you can affirm that God's abiding love will help him see the rainbow—even on the stormiest day.

263

Develop a class mission statement. Your mission statement will help give purpose to your class, especially as busy members become overcommitted with outside obligations and need to refocus from time to time.

264

Exercise self-control. During times when you feel angry or out of control, learn to turn these feelings over to the Lord instead of taking them out on class members. Use the scripture found in Ephesians 4:26 as a guide: "Do not let the sun go down on your anger."

265

Do a journal check. How is your Spiritual Journal? Reread some of the entries made in the past few months. Is personal growth obvious through these writings? Have worries and concerns lessened? Continue to do this check throughout the year.

266

Share talents. Ask members to share their special talents at an upcoming class social. Encourage them to sing, perform a drama, play an instrument, or do a dramatic reading. Award everyone with a frozen yogurt dessert.

267

Give your time. Call a volunteer organization in your community to see if members could help distribute food or clothing one weekend. Your church may also sponsor special programs for the needy, such as a food or clothing drive, and could use extra help.

268

Affirm and encourage. Discussions are most beneficial if the teacher constantly affirms the participants' responses. Adopt the "all is okay" as you encourage each member to speak. Respond with comments such as "very interesting" or "I like that idea." This builds up the individual and provides strength to the total group.

269

Accept others. Accepting others for who they are instead of trying to mold them into persons we want them to be helps eliminate frustration and disappointments. This example of agape or selfless love becomes a reality as we generate acceptance, forgiveness, and growth and place our ultimate faith in God instead of humankind.

270

Create a classroom environment where members can encounter God. There are many people who are faithful to the church and are scholars of the Word. They have stars for perfect attendance in Sunday school and are generous tithers, but they have never really come to grips with the two great commandments of Scripture: "You shall love the Lord your God with all your heart, and with all your soul, and with all your mind, and with all your strength.... You shall love your neighbor as yourself" (Mark 12:30-31).

271

Focus on matters of the heart. When attention falls on secular matters, we forget the essential teaching of our Christian faith: "That which is external deteriorates and decays in time, but that which is internal is eternal." Remember, our inner selves determine our destiny, and it is this inner spirit that we must nourish each day.

272

Watch for silent communication signs in the classroom. A blank stare or harshly spoken words can be the symptoms of a much greater problem. Try to spend time alone with a member who seems to be under stress and really listen to what is going on in his life.

273

Discuss current news stories with class members. What is the Christian response to these stories? Talk about being a Christian in a secular society. What obstacles do members face at work and in the community as they stand up for personal beliefs? How can your class help support members who are having difficulty in standing strong?

274

Look for the good in all God's children. Find something positive to say to members who seem to dwell on the negative aspects of life. Write a short note complimenting them on special talents and attributes.

275

Trust in God. Know that God is guiding you as you make daily decisions regarding your class. This trust stems from an intimate and ongoing prayerful relationship with Jesus Christ. Remember the promise found in Matthew 21:22: "Whatever you ask for in prayer with faith, you will receive."

276

Offer support for a member who is undergoing personal crisis. "A friend loves at all times, and kinsfolk are born to share adversity" (Proverbs 17:17). Believe in this person and be his advocate when personal trials seem overwhelming.

277

Encourage members to seek inner strength. Paul wrote in 1 Timothy 4:8: "While physical training is of some value, godliness is valuable in every way, holding promise for both the present life and the life to come." Just as we can build up our outer body by regular and consistent exercise, so can we strengthen our inner resources by regular and consistent cultivation of our relationship with God.

278

Talk about doubts. When a member expresses doubts about his faith, teach him to seek answers through worship attendance, Bible study, prayer, and Christian fellowship. While doubts are not wrong, allowing doubts to control us is not spiritually healthy. You will become a role model and a living example of God's abiding love as members see you dealing with life's ebb and flow. Let members see examples of "God who is at work in you, enabling you both to will and to work for his good pleasure" (Philippians 2:13).

279

Invite a member to share Sunday dinner with you. It's easy to celebrate Sunday dinner after church—if you plan ahead. Start early in the week by cooking and freezing your main dish. Thaw the food the night before and heat on Sunday morning. With the meal already prepared, you can spend valuable time getting to know your guest.

280

Enjoy your class. Is your class a place for celebration and fellowship? As you live the life set by the example of Christ, may your members see that it is a life of joy, promise, and celebration. Pray that your members say, "Being a Christian was the most exciting thing I ever saw my teacher do!"

281

Be a loving listener. Your reaction to a member's words determines how much he or she will communicate with you in the class. If you come across as unyielding, then the person may feel that it is not worthwhile to talk with you and stop talking altogether. Try to listen to the other person and relate to what he is saying without judgment. Give responses that are fair and reasonable as you open doors to loving communication.

282

Stay centered. All things work together for good for those who love the Lord. Although you will have trials and tribulations as a Sunday school teacher, staying centered on God's abiding love will help see you through difficulties. Remember, there is always a rainbow after the storm. "Blessed is anyone who endures temptation. Such a one has stood the test and will receive the crown of life that the Lord has promised to those who love him" (James 1:12).

283

Recapture your initial enthusiasm for teaching. Remember the drive and enthusiasm you had when you first started teaching? Attitude is crucial in boosting attendance and sharing God's love. Read Romans 12:2, and recapture that "fresh newness" that Paul speaks of, that winning spirit.

284

Continue to seek new members. You can boost your class attendance by inviting newcomers to the area and to your church, nonchurched people currently living in your neighborhood and community, and inactive members in the class and church. Motivate your active members to reach out to all of these people.

285

Focus on the eternal rewards. No one ever said that the Christian life would be easy. Often you will be called upon to make decisions using knowledge you have gained from the Bible, and sometimes this will not be a popular position. You may encounter repercussions from class members. If so, you will not be the first Christian to have experienced this. Keep in mind the eternal rewards as you openly deal with any conflict and continue to study.

286

Become emotionally connected. Go out for dessert with each member, and let him or her choose the place. Sometimes it is easier to talk with people when we are on equal turf instead of at church, where the busyness of classroom activities keeps us distracted.

287

Name spiritual experiences. Ask your members, "What did you see this week that was of God?" Some examples might include a colorful sunrise, the smiles of friends, the new blossoms on flowers or the healing taking place in a co-worker.

288

Share meals together. Plan to meet before worship at a local restaurant and enjoy breakfast (Dutch treat). You can reserve a large table and have your lesson while eating, then go as a group to the services at church.

289

Cultivate your circle of teacher friends. Make plans with other Sunday school teachers for dinner or an outing. Nurture these friendships as you receive helpful information about teaching in the church today. You will find this circle of friends to be supportive and helpful when questions or problems arise.

290

Admit that you don't know. When life seems unfair or tragedy occurs in the life of a member, it is appropriate to tell members that you don't know the answer to why this occurred. However, continually acknowledge that God loves each of us and wants the best for us.

291

Follow the teacher's guide. Prepare a written lesson plan, listing questions you want to ask, ideas you want to discuss, and an introduction and conclusion to your lesson.

292

Answer to a higher calling. As a teacher, you know firsthand what Christians are up against in the world. Yet you also know that no matter what the ethical issues outside of the church, we are all to answer a higher calling. As Christians, this higher calling means that we are summoned to live in the world, but not be of the world. We can experience an abundant life right where we are without giving in to society's secular demands. What demands are made on your members?

293

Change your attitude. Developing an enthusiastic attitude in your teaching ministry is possible. Instead of saying no to new ideas and concepts, ask "Why not?" Often we get too comfortable in our traditions and methods. Remain open to innovative changes in teaching methods, concepts, and structures. Make it a point to try new ways of doing things.

294

Evaluate regularly. Do you need to place more emphasis on creating a welcoming environment in your classroom? Do you need more organization for caring with members helping you write notes or make phone calls each week? Perhaps your class needs to become an "inviting" class. Whatever your needs, make sure that someone has offered to take this on as a project.

295

Stay flexible with your methods, even if attendance decreases. If you arrive on Sunday morning to face just a handful of students, engage them in active research after a brief morning lecture. Give them a problem, then ask them to do individual research and report the answers to the entire group. This research could involve using the Bible to find supportive scriptures for the morning's topic or going to the church library to find answers in various commentaries. Encourage members to take ownership of the material as they search for information.

296

Be accepting. Differences happen even in the most loving Sunday school class. Yet it is when we push and tug against one another that we begin to discover who we are; we begin to grow into the persons God intended. It is when we compassionately reach out to all members "even though . . ." that God will bless our class.

297

Trust in the Holy Spirit. The Holy Spirit is God's heartbeat in our lives—the inner assurance that we are not alone. Read John 14:26 and turn over the fears that block you from being whole.

298

Find favorite verses. The Bible offers great solace to the weary. What favorite verses offer you consolation during times of adversity? Write them down on sticky notes and affix to your refrigerator. Share them with your class members as you teach about inner strength and share a personal relationship with the One who never leaves us alone.

299

Tape your lesson. Make sure homebound members receive audiotapes of your Sunday school lesson, along with the curriculum being studied. A videotape of class members at a social or a service project would also enable the members to feel involved. Be sure to send the weekly bulletin, along with a personal note of encouragement.

300

Be sensitive to all members. When members confide in you, care enough to be sensitive about what is being said, even if it seems irrelevant. Empathize with the speaker. Compassion, sincerity, and empathy communicate your feelings of friendship and support. A relationship that really works and involves personal caring means going that extra mile—together!

301

Accept what each member says. This does not mean that you have to agree with the personal view or opinion, but simply accept what each person says as being valid. This unconditional acceptance relays a caring message as you respect feelings and opinions.

302

Don't give up! If you are anticipating an upcoming slump in attendance due to the holidays or summer vacation, remember this: most of the people will be in town during this time. There are endless ways to creatively touch the lives of these absentee in-town members, including personal evangelism tools, class socials, innovative teaching methods, props, and more. What tools might help your class boost attendance this month?

303

Be creative. Especially when there is a lull in attendance, try to incorporate creative methods such as filmstrips, costumes of biblical times, dramatic role plays, video or audio tapes, background music during teaching, guest lecturers, or maps of ancient Bible times.

304

Be flexible. Change your teaching aids each week to add a sense of anticipation to the next week's class. While a video may be an excellent learning tool, it should not replace a teacher's lecture or discussion every week. A plan that would allow for diversity and increased interest might be to supplement the lessons with a video the first week, pictures of ancient times the second, a Bible scholar to teach the third week, then plotting the travels on maps the fourth.

365

Plan to go out to lunch as a class once each month. Select a reasonably priced restaurant near the church and invite members to bring spouses, children, grandchildren, and friends to this monthly fellowship.

306

Thank God for each member during class prayer time. Periodically, thanking God openly for each member helps affirm his or her importance as a member of the class and as a child of God. During the class prayer time, occasionally lift up each member to God, along with special prayer concerns and affirmations. The simple prayer, "Thank you, God, for *(member's name)*" gives that person a greater feeling of self-worth and spiritual wholeness.

307

Reach out and touch. Can't you visualize our Lord with his arms around children, lifting up the lame, and embracing those in pain? As he preached love and concern, he also demonstrated them. He reached out with gentle, caring hands, touching cold and empty lives with his power. Be sure you have touched the lives of your members in some meaningful way this week.

308

Know yourself. Crucial to a growing Sunday school are evangelistic adults who know themselves, know their particular class, remain flexible, meet the needs of their class, and approach Christ's ministry with a positive sense of adventure. With new lesson twists, closer relationships, and enthusiastic teaching, your class can experience new ways of being "filled with God."

309

Join together in mission. Plan to go on a mission trip together. No matter what the age of your class, mission volunteers come in all ages and work together for a common goal. Check with your pastor for opportunities.

310

Make it public. If only a few people attended the last class social, work on your promotion skills. Publicity is one effective means of communication, which uses such methods as class newsletters (given out monthly or mailed), announcements handed out in class or printed in the church bulletin, phone calls (or a phone chain), posters hung in the classroom, and creative tools (a message written on a balloon and tied to members' chairs on Sunday).

311

Live a Christ-centered life. Remind members that as a Christ-centered person, you see things differently. And because you see things differently, you think differently, you act differently. This gives encouragement to seek God's will in every area of life.

312

Watch criticism. Refrain from being critical, even if a member's idea appears totally irrelevant. Rather, build on each person's idea using a comment such as, "That may be true; can anyone else add another thought?" This acceptance will help keep your class discussion on track and prevent unnecessary embarrassment for the speaker.

313

Make a class scrapbook. Collect pictures taken at class socials and projects and put them in a photo album. Ask members to submit a photograph along with one paragraph telling about their lives. Let one member be in charge of keeping this scrapbook current as new members join. Leave this book in a visible location so it can be enjoyed by all.

314

Be creative when praying. A simple song can serve as a powerful prayer. As can a litany describing feelings about a specific topic which is read by all class members. A passage of scripture can also be read as a prayer that pertains to the lesson. By not limiting the types of prayer, we can expand the ways we talk to God.

315

Continue to reach out. How are you ministering to those who are unable to attend your class because they volunteer during the Sunday school hour (for example, children's and youth teachers, nursery workers, and choir members)? Be sure to include these members in your ongoing mailings and invite them to regular class socials.

316

Take advantage of publicity opportunities. Use opportunities during worship, family night suppers, and other intergenerational gatherings to tell about your class projects, studies, and upcoming social events. Use creative ways of giving this information such as drama, clowning, videos, or slides.

317

Set limits. Scriptures affirm the depths of love with the Great Commandment in the Gospels, "You shall love your neighbor as yourself" (Mark 12:31). If you are full of personal tensions, anxieties, and exhaustion, perhaps you are not spending enough time loving yourself. Drawing limits in your life will enable you to better love and care for those around you.

318

See each day as an opportunity to share God's love. No matter what pressures you are under, you must know that Christ's love is other-centered. Once you have yielded to the love of Christ, this is the way you will act— naturally reaching out to others. Read Matthew 5:16.

319

Allow for imperfection. Expect the best from class members but also allow for human frailty. Remember that the apostle Paul recognized our imperfection: "For we know only in part, and we prophesy only in part; but when the complete comes, the partial will come to an end" (1 Corinthians 13:9-10).

320

Seek guidance in your teaching ministry. Yield yourself to the Lord's ways as you seek specific guidance in your teaching ministry. Keep a prayer list with your curriculum and check off answers to prayer as you give them to the Lord.

321

Expect a miracle. Start each class time in praise, marveling at God's plan for each member as it unfolds before your eyes. Allow time for members to share miraculous ways in which God has touched their lives.

322

Be the class manager. It is easy to stay in lengthy discussions about an upcoming social or have one member dominate the prayer requests for minutes on end. Yet it is also important to remember that members come to class to learn the Word of God. As the teacher, it is your job to manage the group so that learning can take place.

323

See God always. Don't we all yearn for that mountaintop experience, that exhilarating spiritual high that we experienced with other Christians? While making plans to meet with God during class time, realize that he is with you all the time.

324

Continue to be forgiving. The whole principle of the Gospels lies in forgiveness. Yet, who hasn't harbored feelings of anguish after a disagreement in class? Encourage members to continually place their faith in God and to build their lives around God's Word so they can experience the strength to forgive those who are different or who have values that are different. This agape or selfless love becomes a reality as we generate acceptance, forgiveness, and growth, and as we place our ultimate faith in God instead of humankind.

325

Learn from one another. Ask members to bring examples of their hobbies to a class social. Hobbies could include gardening, woodworking, coin and stamp collecting, painting, cooking, and songwriting, as well as others. Encourage members to learn from one another and discover common interests. Talk about the diversity of interests and talents at your next class session.

326

Continue to study. Use your study time to look up the scripture references in various commentaries. Do you understand the meaning of each? Are there other scriptures that would be useful to the lesson? Write these down for classroom use. Call your pastor or other biblical scholar if you need further interpretation of the scriptures being used or if you have theological questions.

327

Provide a job swap. Have members write down their specific hobbies, talents, and interests. Ask a volunteer to post these on a poster board. Encourage members to swap talents as they help one another with specific needs. For example, one member who enjoys yard work may offer to start a garden for someone who enjoys cooking. In turn, the cook might offer to provide baked goods for the gardener.

328

Make lists and files to stay organized. Lists are a valuable planning aid. You can keep lists of members' theological questions that need to be answered. You can also list materials, books, or other items that you will need to use for next Sunday's lesson. Making lists enables you to stay clear mentally as you organize your thoughts and lesson outline.

329

Stay positive. Does a positive atmosphere permeate your class? A group that is secured in God's love through Jesus Christ will be eternal; "a threefold cord is not quickly broken" (Ecclesiastes 4:12). Being a positive teacher is not an easy task, especially as we deal with different personalities in the classroom. Set positive teaching goals with God leading the way.

330

Continue to set goals each week. A lesson goal might be, "To help members understand the unconditional love of God" or "To show members that God's forgiveness is available to all." Be sure to keep these goals in your thoughts and prayers as you look for ways to lead your class into a new awareness of God.

331

Practice a variety of teaching methods. While some teachers prefer the lecture style of teaching, others choose group discussion, research, buzz groups, or small groups. Whatever method of teaching you select, it is important to be innovative. Vary your method from time to time to see which one works best with your class.

332

Meet the needs of your class. Once you become familiar with the material you are to teach, think of your particular class. How can you make this lesson relevant to your members? Are there specific life and faith needs to which this lesson speaks? Look at the writer's suggestions for ways to present the material. Jot down ideas on the outline that you have found useful in teaching that may pertain to the topic. Plot your way through the session and see if you receive the desired outcome.

333

Follow God's call to teach. When we respond to God's call and recognize our inner spirit, our soul, we begin to embrace the true character of our being—the very essence of who we are—and we are able to tackle life's demands, including teaching, with greater enthusiasm. Make plans to revitalize your inner spirit today with a renewed commitment to a devotional life, including prayer, Bible study, and time for listening to God.

334

Draw closer to Christ during turmoil. When trials occur in the classroom that trigger negativity or guilt, it often seems impossible to face another Sunday morning. However, there are no guarantees that we will be insulated from the worst life has to offer. As Christians, we must know that the best in life is always more powerful than the worst. And the best can be experienced right now as decisions are made that draw us all closer to the cross.

335

Don't throw in the towel! So many of us feel that if only we work hard enough, our class will experience growth. We feel that if only we are obedient to God and to one another, then trials in our classes will not come our way. Life doesn't work this way. Although diligence and obedience are necessary for a growing class, there are things that are out of our control. That is where faith comes in, and faith is the conviction that there is One who is in control, whose nature is love.

336

Listen for answers to prayer. Teach class members to take time to be still, to hear God speaking during prayer. Encourage them to keep a paper and pen handy during their daily prayer and devotion time. As they think of specific needs or answers to concerns, ask them to write these down. Often these very thoughts are direct answers to prayer.

337

Talk about Christian values. The cost of being a Christian in a secular world is high, but God demands unconditional surrender to his will. He asks us to do things that take a great deal of effort and that may be painful. Especially when faced with conflicting values, people need to understand that standing strong is what Christians are to do even though it is not easy at the moment.

338

Look for the hope and beauty of our Christian faith in those around you. This involves taking time to appreciate God's world instead of hurrying throughout the day. Meditate on the scripture found in Philippians 4:8: "Whatever is true, . . . think about these things."

339

See hope even when situations seem hopeless. Paul teaches in Philippians 4:13: "I can do all things through him who strengthens me." Our Christian faith is a faith of hope. Realizing the possibility and promise in the difficult times is one of the keys to successful teaching in the Sunday school.

340

Become ambassadors for Christ. Have members reflect on important Christians who influenced their lives in years past. How did these men and women of God make them feel loved? Pray together and thank God that someone cared enough to share the incarnate love of Christ.

341

Celebrate God's grace. Ask class members to share moments from their past when they experienced God's grace.

342

Pause for spiritual reflection. Spend time outdoors. Consider the colors, textures, and scents of God's creation. Reflect on childhood days when you found inner peace and tranquility in God's outdoor kingdom.

343

Talk about tithing. Christian stewardship is a way of life, and Jesus is the perfect example for us to follow. Jesus used every moment of his life to glorify God; we must do the same. Teach your child about tithing and make this her habit as she gives 10 percent to Sunday school offerings. Remind her that "God loves a cheerful giver" (2 Corinthians 9:7).

344

Have a Sunday school exchange. Make plans with a neighboring church or a church with a different ethnic background to meet for Sunday school. Attend worship together, and enjoy lunch if time permits.

345

Talk about witnessing. Ask: Is it easy or difficult to be a Christian witness? Is it possible for members to gain the strength, knowledge, and courage to share their faith in God when peers or co-workers often tear down their very belief? When life situations are difficult? Remind your class of God's everlasting strength.

346

Gain a youthful perspective on life. Ask some of the youth members of the church to serve as classroom teachers on Sunday. Teens can share the message of Jesus Christ from their experiences and can also let you know what projects they are doing to share this message with others. Consider sponsoring youth with financial support for upcoming trips.

347

Seek support from your pastor and church leaders. Studies show that those who have strong social support are healthier and handle stress more effectively. If you need someone to talk to, consider joining a support group at your church or in your community.

348

Remember whose you are. In the midst of understanding that we must be Christlike in our daily actions, we must also discover the connection between what happens on Sunday and what happens the rest of the week. How can you help members to make this connection?

349

Celebrate music. Ask members to list their ten favorite hymns. Select the five hymns that get the most votes, and ask your music director to lead them on Sunday morning. Locate and share historical information about each hymn with your class. Discuss the meaning of the lyrics and how they relate to today's world.

350

Set up a class project day. Plan to work on a much-needed project such as cleaning the classroom, redecorating bulletin boards, or even painting furniture. Go out to lunch or dinner when you are through and talk about your strengths as a class.

351

Recheck your journal. Reread some of the entries made in the past few months. Do you see how God is moving in your life? How has God answered your prayers? Continue to recheck your journal throughout the year.

352

Pace yourself. Recheck your daily calendar, and make sure that all commitments are easily attainable without adding more pressure. If you are feeling rushed or harried, prioritize these commitments, and eliminate any that you can. If you need to take a Sunday off, line up another teacher to substitute ahead of time.

353

Be the spark in your class. It takes only one spark to get a fire going. Tiny sparks of faith can give hope and enthusiasm to the most distressing classroom situations. And it is these sparks that allow teachers to see that the class is becoming energized with the love of Jesus Christ.

354

Be thankful. Giving thanks to those around you is an essential part of our faith. Be sure to take time this week to realize your blessings and acknowledge God's gifts. Reach out in love to class members who have touched your life in some way.

355

Enjoy your members. God made each of us unique: different gifts, talents, and ideas. Appreciate this diversity each time you are at church and thank God for the many gifts.

356

Record your lesson. Take a tape recorder to Sunday school, and record your class session. Listen to your teaching style and the group's response. Did you get the intended message across? What would help you be more effective in delivering the biblical lesson? Did one student dominate the discussion? If so, how could you involve more members next week?

357

Don't ignore your personal friends. Jesus taught, "No one has greater love than this, to lay down one's life for one's friends" (John 15:13). Allow time each day to touch base with close friends.

358

Continue to study the Bible daily. It is important for a teacher to be in study—privately and with others. The Bible offers inspiration, strength, knowledge, and insight into human living and can give a strong background to every Christian who is striving for an "owned" faith.

359

Allow yourself to be "good enough." Some Sunday school teachers are not fulfilled unless they actively play the role of "Super Hero." The reality is that no one can play this role without suffering in some way. Give yourself permission to be "good enough" in some areas.

360

Take time for self-reflection. If you were to be a better Christian, what would need to change? If you were to improve your teaching skills, what should you do? Write down three goals you need to work toward as you strive to strengthen your faith and witness.

361

See God. Look for godly attributes in each class member. Sometimes it is difficult to see any good in disgruntled members who are argumentative. Yet try to see the world as they experience it. Is there a reason for their anger and negativity? Does your belief in them make a difference in how they respond to others?

362

Anticipate change. As creatures of habit, most of us are quite satisfied with the "tried-and-true" in our classes—singing the same hymns, praying at the same time, and sitting by the same members each week. Yet sometimes changes within a class can motivate growth, help newcomers get involved, and open doors for creative spontaneity. Create opportunities for change in your class by rearranging classroom furniture, singing an unknown hymn, or reading a praise litany.

363

Take spiritual risks. Faith is a dynamic, forward-looking relationship with the Creator. However, when we are too careful with our Christian faith, we can miss out on the real exhilaration of life—God's serendipities. We need to stretch, venture out, and take risks as we put our ultimate trust in God.

364

Remember who you are teaching! You are teaching people, not merely a lesson. Stay focused on each individual in your class as you share God's unending love.

365

Go and teach. Jesus' final emphasis in his ministry is to "go therefore and make disciples of all nations" (Matthew 28:18). Jesus' commandment begins with our personal witness in the classroom as we teach to share information, as well as the love of Christ, providing that classroom environment where grace can be experienced and an "owned" faith can be the expected result.